William Bolcom

Sonatina
for Violin and Piano

ISBN 0-634-02608-9

EDWARD B. MARKS MUSIC COMPANY / EXCLUSIVELY DISTRIBUTED BY HAL•LEONARD® CORPORATION

7777 W. BLUEMOUND RD. P.O. BOX 13819 MILWAUKEE, WI 53213

Sonatina
for Violin and Piano

I

William Bolcom
(1958)

Lo stesso tempo

December 9, 1958

II

attacca

Sonatina
for Violin and Piano

I

William Bolcom
(1958)

II

III

10

December 6, 1958 Mills College, Oakland — Seattle